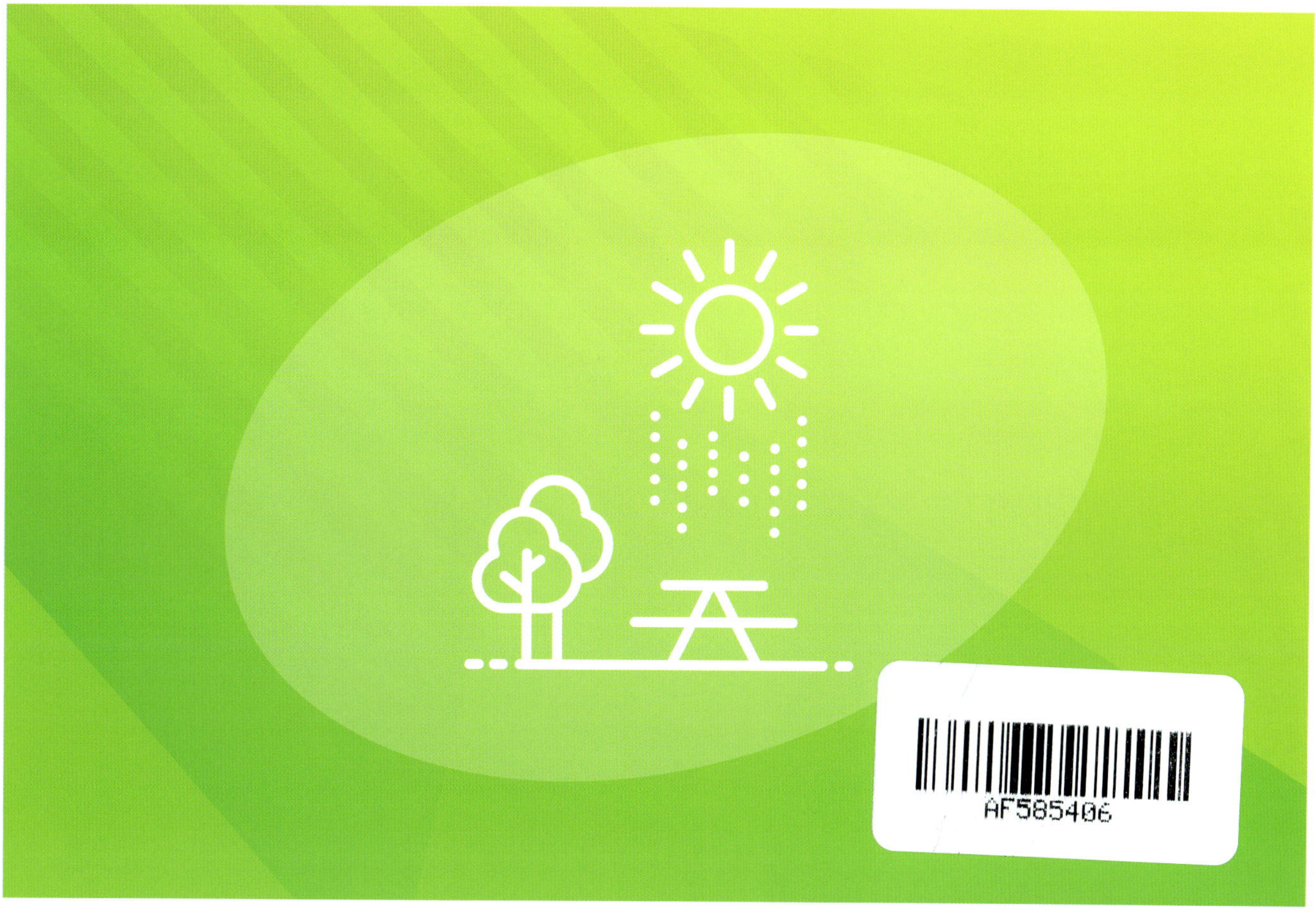

Australia's Environmental Issues

CLIMATE CHANGE

Redback Publishing
PO Box 357 Frenchs Forest NSW 2086
Australia

www.redbackpublishing.com.au
orders@redbackpublishing.com.au

978-1-925860-26-9

Author: Peter Turner
Editor: Michael Anderson
Proofer: Marianne Lindsell
Designer: Redback Publishing

MIX
Paper from responsible sources
FSC® C020056
FSC
www.fsc.org

Original illustrations © Redback Publishing 2019
Originated by Redback Publishing

Printed and bound in China

Acknowledgements
Abbreviations: l—left, r—right, b—bottom, t—top, c—centre, m—middle
We would like to thank the following for permission to reproduce photographs: (Images © shutterstock) p24 Snowy hydro murray 1 machine hall floor - Ear1grey at the English language Wikipedia via Wikimedia Commons.

Every effort has been made to contact copyright holders of any material reproduced in this book. Any omissions will be rectified in subsequent printings if notice is given to the publisher.

NATIONAL LIBRARY OF AUSTRALIA
A catalogue record for this book is available from the National Library of Australia

CONTENTS

INTRODUCTION

THE CHANGING WEATHER

Weather surrounds us all the time. Depending on the weather, we might put on a jumper, or perhaps just shorts and a T-shirt. Although the weather changes every day, it is quite consistent over longer periods, giving us average weather conditions known as climate. In Australia for example, we tend to have mild winters and hot summers, whereas a country in the Northern Hemisphere is more likely to have very cold winters and mild summers. Despite the differences in climate between countries around the world, our planet has an overall average climate. Earth's mild climate ensures that we can grow food, enjoy a sunny day and live our lives without being too concerned by weather conditions.

What is Climate Change?

Climate Change describes the process by which the overall climate moves from one average to a new average. The overall climate has changed radically a number of times over the 4.6 billion years that Earth has existed. This has led to dramatic changes not only in the daily weather, but also to natural structures such as oceans, coastlines and entire continents. Changes in the climate can be caused by internal movements of the planet, such as tectonic plates shifting deep beneath the surface, or external influences such as meteors. Most recently, a new form of climate change has been occurring, and it is caused by humans.

HOW IS THE CLIMATE MEASURED?

Atmospheric science is the study of the atmosphere. The atmosphere is the cloud of gases that surrounds our planet. One branch of atmospheric science is meteorology. The person who reads the weather on TV is a meteorologist. Meteorologists study weather patterns and predict how the weather might change.

Climatology is a branch of atmospheric science concerned with average weather patterns over longer periods of time. Climatologists, or climate scientists, look at these patterns, as well as extreme events such as hurricanes and tidal waves, and predict changes in Earth's overall temperature. The work of meteorologists and climatologists helps to determine how changes in the climate will affect the Earth's environment and its inhabitants.

WHAT IS GLOBAL WARMING?

In recent years, scientists have noticed that Earth's average temperature has been rising. This phenomenon is referred to as global warming. Although it may not seem like a big deal if the temperature rises by a few degrees, it can actually make a huge difference to all sorts of things: rainfall patterns change, sea levels rise and the ice at the north and south poles melts. Scientists and many other people are very concerned that global warming will get much worse unless humans do something about it.

PARTICIPATION IN THE IPCC IS OPEN TO ALL MEMBER COUNTRIES OF THE WORLD METEOROLOGICAL ORGANIZATION (WMO) AND UNITED NATIONS. IT CURRENTLY HAS 195 MEMBERS.

The Intergovernmental Panel on Climate Change

In 1988, the United Nations established the Intergovernmental Panel on Climate Change (IPCC), which is made up of hundreds of the world's top scientists. It is their role to assess the environmental, economic and scientific information on climate change, so that we can better understand what might happen and what needs to be done to prevent it. In a report published in 2007, the scientists stated that warming of the climate system is unequivocal, as is now evident from observations of increases in global air and ocean temperatures, widespread melting of snow and ice and rising average global sea level. This report was updated in 2015, and once again stated that warming of the climate system is unequivocal, and since the 1950s, many of the observed changes are unprecedented over decades to millennia.

The Sun - World's Power Station

The sun's energy sustains all life on Earth. Without the sun, the temperature on Earth would drop to absolute zero (-273 degrees Celsius), the oceans would freeze and nothing would be able to survive. The sun provides the energy for the building blocks of life, including water, oxygen, carbon and photosynthesis (the process by which plants grow). The power of the sun's rays striking the Earth provides as much energy as 173 million power stations working 24 hours a day. The sun is the world's biggest power station.

CLIMATE CHANGE AT A GLANCE

DROUGHTS

Decreases in winter and spring rainfall for Southern continental Australia, with an increase in droughts

SEA-LEVEL

Sea-level rise to continue

RAINFALL

Extreme rainfall events likely to be more intense

FIRE WEATHER

Harsher fire weather projected for Southern and Eastern Australia

FAST FACT

Combining global data sets finds:

- The five warmest years in the global record have all come in the 2010s
- The 10 warmest years on record have all come since 1998
- The 20 warmest years on record have all come since 1995

TEMPERATURE

Temperatures will increase, with more hot days and fewer cool days

CYCLONES

Tropical cyclones projected to decrease in number, but increase in intensity

GLOBAL

Global temperature rise to continue

OCEANS

Oceans around Australia to warm further and acidification will continue

A HISTORY OF CLIMATE CHANGE

The Earth has been around for billions of years and has gone through many changes during that time. There have been ice ages, followed by warmer periods that have given life to numerous creatures, including primitive sea anemones, dinosaurs and eventually humans and the many animals we know today. Now, the planet's temperature is changing again, but this time it is due to human activity rather than natural events.

CONSTANT CLIMATE

Homo sapiens, or humans, have existed on Earth for approximately 200,000 years and have experienced many variations in climate. But, for the last 5,000 years, the overall climate has been similar, with an average temperature of 14 degrees Celsius. This regular temperature has allowed us to grow crops for food and to build homes and entire cities without worrying that extreme weather will force us to move. Humans have come to rely on and even take for granted the consistency in the climate that allows us to live as we do.

Ice Ages

The Earth has experienced four major ice ages, during which much of the planet was covered in thick sheets of ice. During these times, only a few hardy organisms existed. Scientist believe that the last major ice age ended around 10,000 years ago, although there have been minor ice ages since then. Today, there is very little ice on the surface of the planet, and most of it is found at the north and south poles. Yet the Earth's average temperature is only 4 degrees warmer than during the last ice age. So, an overall climate change of only a few degrees can mean the difference between an ice age and a comfortable planet, or even one that is too hot for many life forms.

THE UNIVERSE IN A DAY

To visualise the age of the universe, which includes the sun and all the planets, imagine its entire life up till now as a day of 24 hours. During the incredibly short time, the planet has changed almost as much as during the most extreme periods of climate change in the past.

RECENT WARMING

Something strange has been happening to the overall climate of the planet since 1950. Although 70 years is only the tiniest fraction of the Earth's lifetime, climatologists have found that the average temperature has increased by nearly 1 degree in that time. They are predicting further temperature increases this century, although they are uncertain how great these will be. We already know there will be a 1 or 2 degree increase, but if there are increases of 3 or more degrees there will be serious consequences for many people. For example, people living along coastlines may need to move because of rising water levels, and many plant and animal species may become extinct because they cannot adapt to the changing climate.

LIFETIME OF PLANET EARTH

4.6 BILLION YEARS AGO
EARTH BEGINS

2 BILLION YEARS AGO
ATMOSPHERE FORMS

1.5 BILLION YEARS AGO
SIMPLE ORGANISMS APPEAR

200 MILLION YEARS AGO
DINOSAURS APPEAR

2 MILLION YEARS AGO
HUMAN-LIKE ANCESTORS APPEAR

200 000 YEARS AGO
EARLY HUMANS WALK THE EARTH

10 000 YEARS AGO
LAST MAJOR ICE AGE ENDS

5000 YEARS AGO
TEMPERATURE STABILISES AT 14 C

WHAT IS CAUSING GLOBAL WARMING?

Global warming is created by complex changes in the atmosphere, which are caused by increases in greenhouse gases. These increases are caused by human activities, including using electricity, driving cars and many other things we take for granted.

The Atmosphere

The atmosphere acts like a tent or greenhouse, protecting the Earth from extreme levels of the sun's radiation, known as ultraviolet (UVB) radiation, as well as other cosmic particles. The atmosphere also traps enough sunlight and heat to keep Earth's surface temperature warm and suitable for life. It is made up of mixed layers of gases, including carbon dioxide, methane, hydrogen, nitrogen and oxygen. Without the atmosphere, the heat from the sun would beam directly on to the planet and make it far too hot for any life to exist.

Greenhouse Gases

Greenhouse gases are invisible and without odour, yet they surround us and make up the atmosphere. They have kept the Earth's temperature constant for the past 5000 years. When more and more greenhouse gases become part of the atmosphere, however, more heat is trapped and the Earth's overall temperature rises. This is commonly known as the greenhouse effect.

Australia's Emissions

Australia has a relatively small population approaching 25 million people, yet we are putting millions of tonnes of greenhouse gases into the atmosphere each year. New Environment Department figures shows gas emissions grew by 0.7 per cent in 2017. The previous year gas emissions grew 0.8 per cent. Because fossil fuels provide most of our energy needs, Australia's emissions are extremely high per person. But, because of our small population, our total emissions represent only 1.3 per cent of the world's emissions. The biggest polluting countries, overall, are China, the USA and India.

FOSSIL FUELS

Greenhouse gasses occur naturally in the atmosphere, and are also generated by humans when we burn fossil fuels such as coal, gas and petroleum. Fossil fuels are essentially the remains of plants and animals that died millions of years ago. When these fuels are burned, the carbon that has been stored in them is released into the atmosphere, which increases the level of greenhouse gases. The levels of two greenhouse gasses, carbon dioxide and methane, have drastically increased in recent times. This has caused the atmosphere to retain too much heat, which in turn has created global warming.

THE EARTHS ATMOSPHERE

FAST FACT
Humans have been burning fossil fuels since the beginning of the Industrial Revolution in the 1800s.

Over two-thirds of the radiation from the sun is absorbed by the Earth, or becomes part of the water cycle. The rest is reflected back into space.

EXOSPHERE
>700-190.000 km

THERMOSPHERE
80-700 km

MESOSPHERE
50-80 km

STRATOSPHERE
12-50 km

OZONE LAYER
20-30 km

TROPOSPHERE
0-12 km

BIOSPHERE

The mesosphere is the layer directly above the stratosphere. It is located more than 50 kilometres above the Earth's surface.

The ozone layer is part of the stratosphere. It acts like a shield, absorbing UVB radiation.

The stratosphere is the top layer of the atmosphere. It acts like a lid, keeping all the air and clouds close to the ground.

The troposphere contains all the clouds. 'Tropo' means turning over, this layer is constantly changing.

The biosphere is the part of the Earth that supports life. It is made up of the land, ice and oceans on the planet.

CFCs

Chlorofluorocarbons, or CFCs, are used in aerosol cans, fridges, foam and some air conditioners. They are extremely potent and can heat the atmosphere up to 15,000 times more than carbon dioxide.

In 1984, scientists discovered that the ozone layer, which is part of the atmosphere, was depleted so badly that there was hardly any ozone left over Antarctica. After widespread concern about the destructive power of CFCs, the world's government signed a treaty in 1987 to eliminate them. Since then, the total consumption of CFCs has decreased by 90 per cent.

Although the 'hole' in the ozone is now shrinking, it is still present over southern Australia, New Zealand and Antarctica, which means that levels of dangerous UVB radiation are higher in these places.

THE EFFECTS OF CLIMATE CHANGE

Average temperatures are increasing around the world, and recently we have experienced some of the hottest days and years on record. In addition, extreme weather events have been occurring more frequently. Scientists believe these events are signs of climate change, and that further changes are to come. Most are expected to occur before the end of the century unless we can halt global warming.

In Australia

As average temperatures increase, Australia will have less rainfall, and the rain will be heavier and more damaging when it comes. We can also expect long-term damage to our coral reefs, coasts, rainforests, wetlands and alpine areas. We will have more hot days and fewer cool days, and there may no longer be snow in winter. Extreme weather events such as floods, tornadoes and heatwaves are likely to be more frequent. More people will be exposed to tropical diseases such as malaria, and many more will die from the effects of heat.

Drought

As the driest continent on Earth, Australia has experienced many droughts, with more extreme drought conditions expected, with even less rainfall. This may affect our ability to grow crops and farm livestock, forcing many farmers off the land. Bushfires will also become an increasingly persistent problem.

Extinction

By the end of the century, three out of five plant and animal species may be extinct due to their inability to cope with rapid environmental change, leaving us with far fewer plants and animals than when humans first walked the Earth. Many countries are collecting seed samples from their plants and putting them somewhere safe, so that we will still have seeds if plants do become extinct.

FORESTS

Trees and other plants store carbon dioxides from the atmosphere in their wood, branches and leaves. Because of this, they are often called carbon sinks. While trees are very helpful in preventing further global warming, they release their stored carbon dioxide back into the atmosphere when they are chopped down or burned. At this point, they add to global warming. Deforestation is the term used to describe the widespread culling of trees.

ICE CAPS AND OCEANS

The ice at the north and south poles is already melting due to warmer air and sea temperatures. When ice melts into the oceans, the volume of water increases, causing sea levels to rise. This is of great concern to many people, and not just those who live near the coast. For example, if the sea level were to rise by 1 metre, about 50 per cent of Bangladesh in South Asia would be flooded, leaving millions homeless.

POSITIVE FEEDBACK CYCLES

Carbon dioxide remains in the atmosphere for about 100 years, so today we are feeling the effects of gases that were released a long time ago. This is of great concern to scientists, along with positive feedback cycles or loops, which are created when an increase in temperature causes events that lead to further increases in temperature, (a vicious cycle). For example, the melting of the ice caps causes sea temperature to rise causing an accelerated melting of the ice caps, and so on. Positive feedback cycles therefore could make global warming far worse than initially predicted.

The Stern Review

The important British report, released in 2006, detailed the economic impacts of climate change and suggested ways of controlling global warming. The report found that: 'The scientific evidence is now overwhelming: climate change is a serious global threat, and it demands an urgent global response... Climate change will affect the basic elements of life for people around the world - access to water, food production, health, and the environment. Hundreds of millions of people could suffer hunger, water shortages and coastal flooding as the world warms.'

In an interview in 2013, Stern said, 'Looking back, I underestimated the risks. The planet and the atmosphere seem to be absorbing less carbon than we expected, and emissions are rising pretty strongly. Some of the effects are coming through more quickly than we thought then in the 2006 Review.' He now believes we are '...on track for something like four degrees.'

The Great Barrier Reef

This reef that stretches for 2000 kilometres along the Queensland coastline is home to more than 400 types of coral, 1500 species of fish and 4000 species of mollusc. It is also a World Heritage site, which means it has outstanding importance to humanity.

Nevertheless, it could be irreparably damaged by two impacts of global warming: coral bleaching and ocean acidification. Rising ocean temperatures damage coral, sometimes permanently, and increased levels of carbon dioxide in the ocean negatively affect many sea creatures. A significant loss of coral and fish species has occurred on the Great Barrier Reef. By 2050, there may be very little live coral left on an important Australian icon.

TRANSPORT EMISSIONS

Most of us take the family car for granted, and do not stop to think that cars, trucks and other vehicles all emit greenhouse gases. Trucks are constantly on the road transporting goods around the world, buses and trains provide public transport. By 2017, there were more than 18.8 million registered passenger cars in Australia. Emissions are at a record high, with a rise in the use of diesel and aviation fuel. Transport is the third largest sector contributing to Australia's greenhouse gas emissions.

Petrol

Currently, most vehicles are powered by petrol, which is created from refined petroleum. Petroleum is a fossil fuel that is found deep beneath the earth and oceans. Refining petroleum, transporting it to fuel stations, and then using it in our vehicles generates enormous amounts of greenhouse gases.

Alternatives to Petrol

Some cars and trucks run on fuels that are better for the environment. Diesel, has higher emissions than petrol per litre, but is used more efficiently in engines, so results in lower emissions overall. Liquid petroleum gas (LPG) is a natural gas that can be used in cars. Even though it is a fossil fuel, it also produces fewer emissions than petrol overall. Other fuels such as ethanol and bio-diesel, which are created from plants such as sugar cane and corn, also produce far fewer emissions.

PUBLIC TRANSPORT

Trains, buses and light rail (trams) do generate greenhouse gas emissions, but they can carry many more people than the average family car. So, emissions per person from these forms of transport are significantly less than from cars. Currently, the only totally emissions-free forms of transport are walking or riding a bicycle.

AIR TRAVEL

Aeroplanes use a special type of fuel called kerosene, which is based on petroleum. In flight, planes produce not only carbon dioxide, but also water vapour and nitrogen. This results in a warming effect nearly three times greater than if these emissions were released at groundlevel. In 2016, national representatives at the International Civil Aviation Organization, ICAO agreed that from 2020 greenhouse gasses will be limited, and any increase in airline CO_2 emissions will be offset by activities like tree planting, which soak up CO_2. Airlines are also striving for more efficient planes and fuel. In 2017, a Qantas plane powered partly by mustard seeds became the world's first biofuel flight between Australia and the United States. Air travel accounts for 2.5 per cent of all carbon dioxide emissions.

ARS OF THE FUTURE

ybrid cars, which use a combination f petrol and an electric engine, use ss than half the petrol of the average ar. Australia is well behind in the obal move toward electric vehicles, hich have much lower emissions than etrol powered cars. They run on an ectric battery, which can be plugged to the electricity grid overnight to charge. The electricity these cars use ostly come from renewable sources.

International Agreements

The Kyoto Protocol was an international agreement that aimed to reduce global warming. It was coordinated by the United Nations in Kyoto, Japan in 1997. When the Kyoto Protocol's first stage came to an end in 2012, it was agreed to extend the period to 2020. However, only 88 of the original Kyoto Protocol signatories accepted and 144 countries were needed for the amendment to go into force. Then in December 2015, 195 countries came together and promised to reduce their carbon emissions over time by signing the Paris Climate Agreement. On June 1st, 2017 President Trump withdrew the U.S. from the Paris Agreement, although that won't be formal until 2020.

WHAT WE EAT

You may be surprised to learn that producing food significantly contributes to global warming. Agriculture represents 16 per cent of total greenhouse gas emissions in Australia. These emissions come from the impact of farming on the land, as well as the methane produced by livestock. Although we all need to eat and cannot completely eradicate agricultural emissions, we do need to find ways to reduce them. By 2020 agriculture emissions are predicted to be 5 per cent higher than in 2017.

Livestock Farming

Grazing animals, including cows and sheep, produce a greenhouse gas called methane as they digest their food. This is released into the atmosphere when they expel gas. Methane is also released from the animals' manure. It may seem surprising, but methane emissions from livestock make up the majority of Australia's emissions from the agricultural sector. Methane can also be found in wet swamps and other damp places such as rubbish tips.

METHANE, WHILE NOT AS COMMON AS CARBON DIOXIDE, IS A VERY POTENT GREENHOUSE GAS AND IS SOMETIMES THOUGHT TO BE EVEN MORE DANGEROUS THAN CARBON DIOXIDE IN LARGE QUANTITIES.

CROP GROWING

Nitrogen is a greenhouse gas that is naturally present in the atmosphere, as well as in soils and water. The artificial fertilisers farmers use on their crops deplete the soil of nitrogen, which becomes nitrous oxide in the atmosphere and adds to the greenhouse effect. Nitrous oxide is not the only greenhouse gas that results from growing crops. Farming machinery and equipment, such as tractors and harvesters, release carbon dioxide when they are used to spread fertilisers and harvest crops, and so do the vehicles that transport agricultural products around the country.

FOOD MILES

The phrase 'food miles' is used to describe the distance that food has travelled to arrive at our table. In the supermarket you can find tomatoes from Italy, asparagus from Peru and orange juice from Brazil. The emissions produced in getting this food to us - by plane, truck or boat - are significant and add to the agricultural emissions from producing the food itself. Eating food that has been grown or made close to where you live reduces food miles and therefore greenhouse gas emissions.

CHOPPING DOWN TREES TO MAKE LAND AVAILABLE FOR AGRICULTURE ALSO RELEASES CARBON DIOXIDE INTO THE ATMOSPHERE.

IMPACT ON FARMING

The long-term impact of global warming will be strongly felt by the agricultural industry and may diminish Australian farmers' ability to provide us with food. By 2030, rising temperatures and a lack of rainfall will make it harder to grow crops, reducing food production in southern and eastern Australia. The extreme heat will also make life much tougher for the sheep, cattle and pigs on Australian farms, with water and feed shortages a problem. Both crops and livestock may also be more exposed to pests and diseases.

Food Waste

In Australia, the household and industrial waste that goes to landfill generates 13 million tonnes of greenhouse gas emissions each year. Some of this waste is food that is left over from meals or has gone bad before being eaten. Many people are not aware that this waste contributes to global warming, but, in fact, waste breaking down in landfill releases methane into the atmosphere. Sometimes, the methane emissions from landfill waste, or biomass, are captured and used to produce renewable energy.

PRODUCING ELECTRICITY IN AUSTRALIA

Energy supplies us with heat and light, and it powers our televisions and provides us with hot water. Energy is created by electricity, which can come from either renewable or non-renewable sources. The majority of the world's electricity comes from burning coal and gas, which are non-renewable and produce large amounts of greenhouse gases. Finding good alternative sources of fuel for producing electricity is one of the greatest challenges in halting global warming.

What is Electricity?

Electricity results from the movement of charged particles called electrons and protons. They create a current of electricity that can be channelled through an electrical conductor (usually a metal wire) and used as energy. Electricity can flow as a direct current (DC), which flows in one direction, or an alternating current (AC), which flows both backwards and forwards. Electricity only flows closed loops or circuits. When we turn off a light, we break the closed circuit s that electricity cannot flow. When we flick the switch on again, the current flow through the circuit and the electricity lights up the bulb.

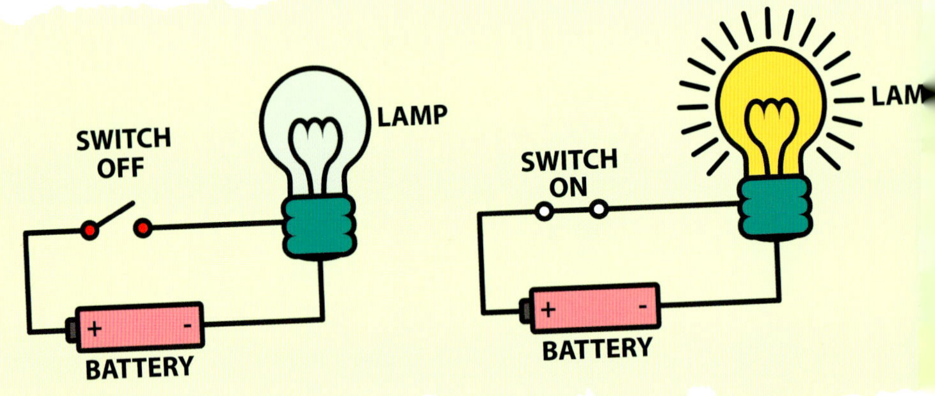

The Electricity Grid

Most of our electricity is produced at power plants that generate huge amounts of energy, and then transfer it to our homes through a grid of wires known as the electricity grid. Our houses are hooked up to this grid. When we turn on the television, for example, the electrical current flows through the wires and powers it up. Some houses in very isolated areas are not hooked up to the electricity grid, so they have to generate their own electricity on site.

FAST FACT

It is estimated that some fossil fuels, such as petroleum, will run out during this or the next century. More than 90 per cent of Australia's electricity is generated from burning coal in large power plants.

GREENHOUSE GAS EMISSIONS

Fossil fuels are natural resources that were created millions of years ago and so are not renewable - once they run out, we will not be able to make any more. Fossil fuels contain carbon, which is released when they are burned, becoming carbon dioxide in the atmosphere. Although burning fossil fuels is a good way to generate electricity, doing so produces huge amounts of greenhouse gas emissions, thus contributing to global warming.

Sources of Electricity

lectricity can come from either renewable or on-renewable sources. Renewable sources include unlight and wind, which are plentiful, but are not urrently used in large quantities. The majority of ustralia's electricity comes from burning fossil fuels uch as coal and gas, which are mined and then urned in large power plants. Burning fossil fuels reates steam, which is used to power large turbines r windmills and make electricity. The electricity is en sent out through the grid to our homes.

ATURAL GAS

ome of our energy is sourced from a fossil fuel called natural gas. This is an odourless, olourless gas that has formed beneath the ocean or land in a similar way to coal. The main gredient of natural gas is the greenhouse gas methane.

Natural gas is transported to our homes through large underground pipelines. Among other things, it can be used to heat water and provide heat for cooking. Because natural gas has no smell, gas companies add sulphur, which has a 'rotten egg' smell, so that if it is leaking in your home you can detect it.

When chilled to cold temperatures, natural gas becomes a liquid that can be used in places where people are not connected to the gas pipelines, or as fuel for vehicles. Burning natural gas produces 30 per cent less greenhouse gas emissions than burning coal.

ALTERNATIVE ENERGY: SOLAR POWER

Solar power is one of a number of alternative energies used in Australia and comes from something we have in plentiful supply: the energy of the sun. The sun's rays can be turned into electricity directly using solar or photovoltaic (PV) panels, or indirectly from steam generators that use the sun to heat a fluid and produce steam, to create solar thermal energy. Currently, most solar energy is generated using PV panels.

How it Works

PV panels are flat reflective panels made up of many small solar cells that convert the sun's energy directly into electricity. Sunlight is made up of photons, which are small particles of solar energy. When photons strike a PV panel, some of them are absorbed, which causes electrons on each solar cell to travel to the front of the cell. This imbalance of energy creates a voltage similar to the negative and positive energy of a battery and generates electricity.

PV panels are placed on north-facing roofs to maximise the amount of sunlight they receive. They can provide all the energy needs of a household. The panels can operate independently of the electricity grid, or they can be hooked up to the central supply in case there is not enough sunlight.

THE TOP TEN SOLAR PRODUCING COUNTRIES GLOBALLY ARE:

1. CHINA
2. JAPAN
3. GERMANY
4. USA
5. ITALY
6. UK
7. INDIA
8. FRANCE
9. AUSTRALIA
10. SPAIN

WHO USES IT?

In Australia, solar increased 10-fold between 2009 and 2011, and quadrupled between 2011 and 2016. Thirty new solar farms were approved in New South Wales and Queensland in 2017, which led to an unprecedented boom in solar panel sales in early 2018.

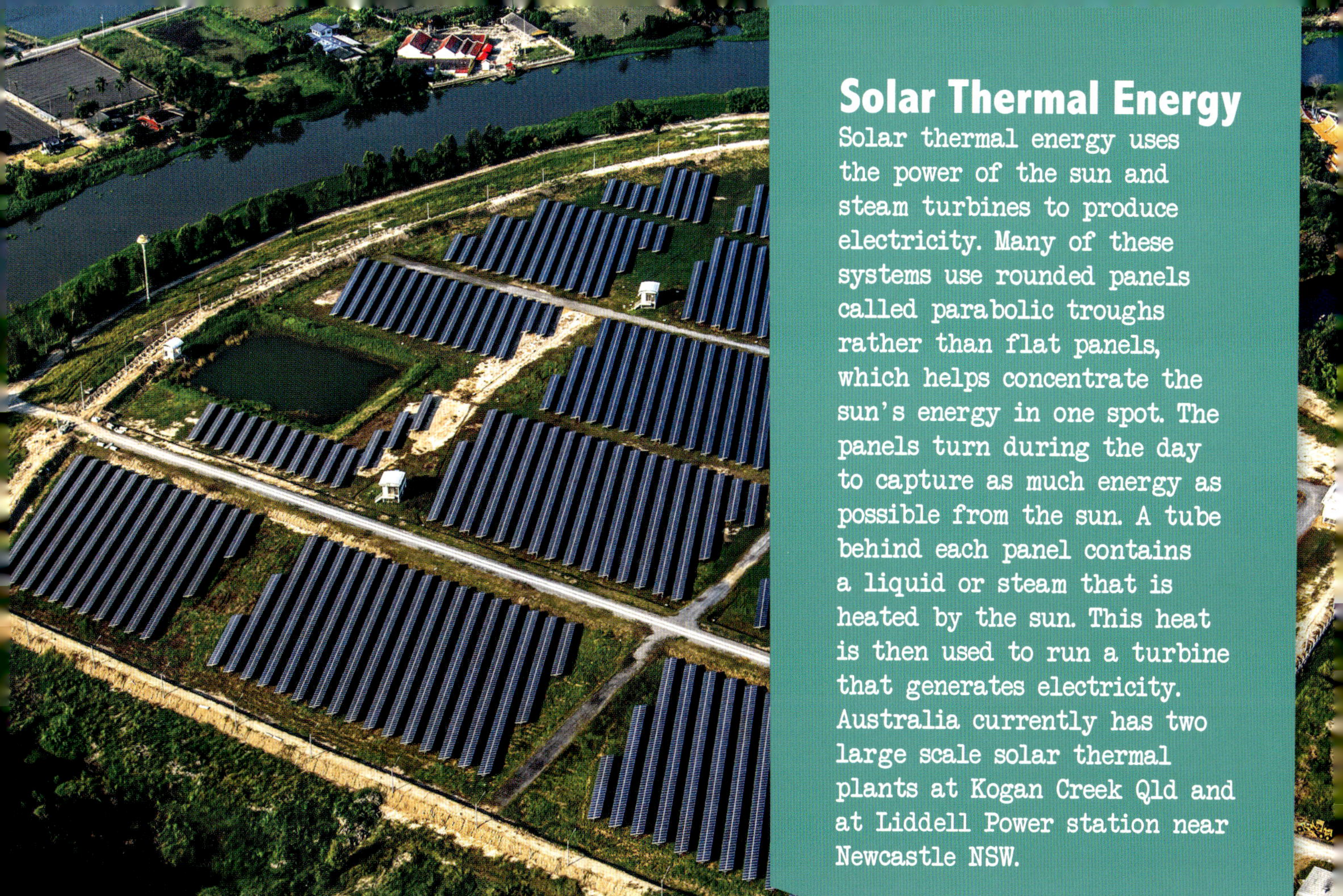

Solar Thermal Energy

Solar thermal energy uses the power of the sun and steam turbines to produce electricity. Many of these systems use rounded panels called parabolic troughs rather than flat panels, which helps concentrate the sun's energy in one spot. The panels turn during the day to capture as much energy as possible from the sun. A tube behind each panel contains a liquid or steam that is heated by the sun. This heat is then used to run a turbine that generates electricity. Australia currently has two large scale solar thermal plants at Kogan Creek Qld and at Liddell Power station near Newcastle NSW.

SUMMING UP

POSITIVES

- Solar energy produces no greenhouse gas emissions or pollution.
- Energy from the sun is free and available most days.
- PV panels allow people to produce their own electricity and be completely self-reliant, rather than having to depend on the electricity grid.

NEGATIVES

- Solar energy is currently more expensive than standard fossil fuel-based electricity because of the high cost of constructing PV panels.
- Solar energy is dependent on the sun's energy and therefore is not available at night or on rainy or overcast days.
- To collect solar energy on a large scale requires a large area of PV panels, which some people feel spoils the appearance of the environment.

ALTERNATIVE ENERGY: WIND POWER

Humans have used windmills for thousands of years to pump water and grind wheat into flour, and today we can use the wind to generate electricity. Wind energy is free and creates no pollution, and the supply of wind is limitless, although strong winds are needed to produce power.

How it Works

Wind power is generated on wind farms, where rows of giant windmills called turbines capture the wind. Farms are often found along coastlines or at sea where the wind is at its strongest. They may also be spread out along a stretch of land to try to ensure a constant supply of wind. The wind must be blowing at 8 metres per second or faster for a turbine to work effectively. When the wind blows, the turbine rotates, which in turn moves a motor that generates electricity. The electricity is fed into a central location on the farm, then connected to the central electricity grid.

WHO USES IT?

Globally, there are about 250,000 wind turbines. China leads the world in wind power, with a capacity greater than the entire European Union, and double the United States, the second largest producer of wind energy.

In Australia, over 30 per cent of Australia's clean energy is produced by wind farms, or 5.3 per cent of the country's overall electricity. Wind energy is the country's fastest growing renewable energy source for electricity production.

In 2019, Australia's largest wind farm will open 250 kilometres northwest of Brisbane. 123 wind turbines will produce around 1.51 million-megawatt hours of renewable energy every year, or enough to power around 260,000 homes. This would cut CO2 emissions by 1.18 million tonnes annually.

Crookwell Wind Farm, New South Wales

The wind farm at Crookwell has been running since 1998. It was the first wind farm in Australia to connect to the central electricity grid. Its eight turbines harness wind energy coming off the Great Dividing Range. It can supply up to 5 megawatts of power at a time, which is enough to provide electricity for 3500 homes. The wind farm saves approximately 8000 tonnes of greenhouse gas emissions a year.

Wave Energy

The energy of waves can be harnessed to generate electricity, however, there are technical difficulties in capturing their energy, including the corrosive impact of salt water on machinery. Wave energy is usually produced by forcing the waves into a narrow channel to increase their size. The power of the waves turns large turbines, which generates electricity.

There are around 200 wave energy devices in different stages of development. Current research indicates that wave energy could produce up to 11 per cent of Australia's energy.

WAVE ENERGY DEVICES

SUMMING UP

POSITIVES

- Wind turbines produce no greenhouse gases or air pollution.
- Modern turbines are quiet, with their noise about the same as background urban noise.
- Wind power has few ongoing running costs.
- Wind energy is the country's fastest growing renewable energy source for electricity production.
- Wind energy will never run out.

NEGATIVES

- If the wind is not blowing, it is not possible to generate electricity.
- Wind power generally needs to be used in addition to other power sources.
- Wind farms need to be built in windy areas, such as along coastlines, where residents may not want wind farms.

HYDRO-ELECTRICITY

Hydro-electricity is the most common form of renewable energy. It uses the power of moving water to generate electricity. Hydro energy has been used by humans for thousands of years, since water was first used to turn a wheel and generate power. Hydro energy has been used in Australia for many years; the Snowy Mountains Hydro Scheme is our most famous hydro-electric power station.

How it Works

Hydro-electric power plants must be located on water channels, where they harness the flow of water in order to create energy. Power is generated by blades or turbines that are rotated by the flowing water. The turbines are hooked up to an alternator, which converts the rotational energy of the turbines into electricity. The electricity is then conveyed to towns and cities through the electricity grid. The amount of energy that can be produced depends on the strength of the water flow. Mountainous regions, where there are rapid water flows and not many people, are among the best places to produce hydro-electricity. Hydro-electricity often involves diverting the water flow, thus permanently transforming rivers into lakes and dams.

The Snowy Mountains Hydro Scheme

The Snowy Mountains Hydro Scheme in southern New South Wales took 25 years to build and was completed in 1974. It is one of the largest and most complex hydro schemes in the world, but most of it is underground and not visible from land. The station collects and stores water that would normally flow downriver, diverting it into 16 large dams and through 145 kilometres of tunnels and nine power stations. The largest dam, Lake Eucumbene, holds nine times more water than Sydney Harbour!

WHO USES IT?

China leads the world with hydropower, followed by the USA, Brazil then Canada. However countries like Ecuador, Ethiopia and Vietnam are making huge progress.

In Australia, there are 120 hydro-electric power stations, with a total capacity of 8,800 megawatts of electricity. The Snowy Mountains Hydro Scheme and the Tasmanian Hydro-electric Corporation together produce about 80 per cent of Australia's hydro-electric power. In 2017, the government announced a $2 billion expansion plan for the Snowy Hydro Scheme, which could add 50 per cent to its capacity.

Biomass Energy

Biomass is organic material made from plant and animal matter, including garbage and other landfill waste. Biomass stores energy from the sun, including gases such as carbon dioxide and methane. Rather than being allowed to escape into the atmosphere, where it adds to global warming, biomass can be turned into bio energy. Biomass currently accounts for around 10 per cent of the world's energy, mostly in poorer countries.

In Australia, there are a number of small, local biomass generators, and sugar cane waste, known as bagasse, is used to produce electricity in sugar mills. It currently accounts for 1 per cent of Australia's electricity, and 7 per cent of renewable electricity production.

SUMMING UP

POSITIVES

- No greenhouse gases are emitted at the hydro power plant, nor is there any air or water pollution.
- Hydro-electricity can be generated quickly, so it can be very useful at peak electricity times, such as first thing in the morning and at night.
- The water needed to generate hydro-electricity can also be used for other needs, such as irrigation.
- Very few people are needed to operate and maintain a hydro power station.

NEGATIVES

- Hydro power plants do have a negative effect on the natural environment, in particular the natural water flow, and may cause rivers to lose significant amounts of water.
- In Australia's drought-affected regions, hydro power plants can divert water away from other needs, such as crop irrigation.
- Hydro-electricity power plants are very expensive to build.

IS NUCLEAR THE ANSWER?

Nuclear power is potentially a major source of energy in Australia, but many people argue that the risks are too great. Nuclear power uses as its source material a natural element called uranium, which Australia has in large quantities.

The Nuclear Cycle

The nuclear power cycle begins with the mining of uranium, which is then processed into enriched uranium-235. The uranium-235 atoms are split in a nuclear reactor at a nuclear power plant by a process called nuclear fission. This process creates incredible amounts of energy - weight for weight, uranium creates 3 million times more power than coal. This energy is harnessed in the form of heat or steam, which is used to drive a turbine and produce electrical power. This is then distributed through the electricity grid.

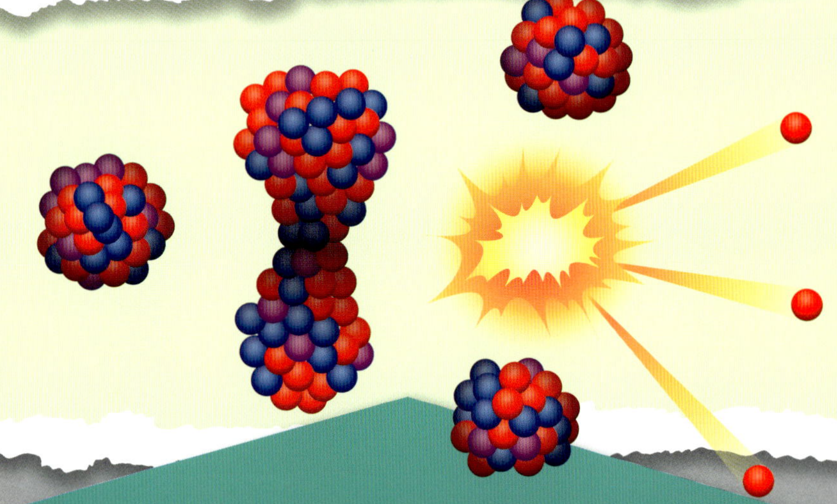

RADIATION AND NUCLEAR WASTE

The process of nuclear fission produces gamma radiation, which is similar to the energy produced from an X-ray. Gamma radiation can penetrate many surfaces, including the human body. High levels cause nausea, vomiting and loss of hair and teeth, and increase the chance of developing cancer. Radiation left over from creating nuclear power is called radioactive waste. It is highly dangerous, remaining radioactive for more than 10,000 years. It must be disposed of safely, and is usually buried deep beneath the ground or sea.

Chernobyl

In 1986, the worst ever nuclear accident occurred at the Chernobyl power plant in the former USSR, now Ukraine. Operators disconnected some safety circuits to do tests on the reactor, which made it unstable. When they tried to put the circuits back, a huge amount of nuclear energy was released, causing a series of explosions. Radioactive material was thrown out of the building into the surrounding areas, and was spread throughout Europe by wind and rain. There were significant levels of radioactivity within 50 kilometres of the reactor, and the official death toll was 3600 people. The United Nations estimates that 5 million people in Europe were exposed to some degree of radioactive contamination from Chernobyl. Many countries stopped building nuclear power plants after the accident, but the nuclear industry has also developed new, far safer reactors.

WHO USES IT?

Nuclear power currently provides 11 per cent of the world's electricity, from about 450 power reactors. Fifty countries produce nuclear energy, and 16 of these depend on it for at least one-quarter of their electricity. France obtains three-quarters of its power from nuclear energy, while Hungary, Slovakia and Ukraine get more than half from nuclear. Currently, Australia has no nuclear power plants.

Fukushima

In March 2011, a massive earthquake in Japan triggered a devastating tsunami. The tsunami disabled the power supply and cooling of three Fukushima Daiichi reactors, causing a nuclear accident. There is much debate about the official information provided to the public about the ongoing health and environmental impact this accident had. The official line is that there have been no changes in radiation levels, which remain safe. Many researchers refute this, stating there are not only high levels of radiation in Japan, but the ocean too has been affected.

In the past up to 30 per cent of Japan's electricity came from nuclear but as of 2016 it had dropped to 2 per cent.

SUMMING UP

POSITIVES

- Nuclear power can produce huge amounts of electricity.
- Nuclear power plants create no greenhouse gas emissions.
- Australia has large amounts of uranium, the base fuel for nuclear power.
- When a nuclear power plant is set up, the running costs are low.
- Nuclear power is supported by some scientists, such as British scientist James Lovelock, who has said, 'Only nuclear power can now halt global warming'.

NEGATIVES

- Building nuclear power plants uses enormous amounts of energy and creates significant greenhouse gas emissions.
- Plants need to be built close to cities, but most people do not want a nuclear power plant built near them.
- Uranium is a limited resource, so nuclear is never going to be the total solution to our power needs.
- Uranium mining takes a huge toll on the natural environment, and most of Australia's uranium is found in environmentally significant areas, such as Kakadu National Park.

YOU AND ME

You will have realised by reading this book that we all contribute to greenhouse gas emissions as we go about our daily lives. Household emissions make up 12 per cent of Australia's total emissions and add around 100 million tonnes of carbon dioxide and methane to the atmosphere each year.

Our Carbon Footprint

Australians are among the biggest carbon polluters in the world. According to the World Bank, we are each responsible for around 19 tonnes of carbon dioxide emissions every year, compared with the average person in the world, who contributes less than quarter of that amount. The amount of emissions we are responsible for is called our carbon footprint.

Australians' emissions are very high for a number of reasons, including our heavy reliance on coal for electricity; our sprawling cities that require high car usage; and our big houses, which require a great deal of energy to run.

Transport

The excessive use of cars significantly contributes to Australia's greenhouse gas emissions. Riding a bike or walking on shorter journeys generates zero emissions. Taking public transport on longer trips reduces our greenhouse gas emissions from transport.

FAST FACT

Australia's healthcare system contributes more than 7 per cent of the country's carbon footprint.

ELECTRICITY

We can significantly reduce the energy consumed by checking the energy rating of new appliances, unplugging unused appliances, and turning off lights. Switching to energy saving globes, which use less electricity than standard bulbs. We can also ensure that our electricity comes from renewable sources by buying it from an accredited 'green power' supplier. Thus both increases investment in renewable energy sources, such as wind and solar power, and reduces our reliance on coal.

FOOD

Livestock such as cows and sheep release huge amounts of methane into the environment. In addition, trees are cleared to provide pasture for these grazing animals. We can reduce the demand for livestock animals and reduce their impact on the planet by eating less meat and dairy products. We can also reduce transport emissions by eating foods that have been grown locally rather than those that have to be transported long distances, and we can support local farmers by shopping at farmers' markets rather than the supermarket. We can also grow our own herbs, fruit and veggies. You cannot get more local than that!

RECYCLING AND COMPOSTING

Food scraps account for more than 40 per cent of household rubbish. They end up as landfill, giving off methane and carbon as they break down. Compost bins and worm farms significantly reduce the amount of waste going to landfill, and at the same time help create rich soil for our plants. Recycling everything you can - including paper, plastics, glass, aluminium cans and steel lids - will also help reduce landfill waste.

Ten easy ways to help reduce global warming

1. Turn the lights off when you leave a room.
2. Turn the TV or computer off at the wall when you are finished with them.
3. Ride your bike or walk rather than getting into the car.
4. Eat foods that have been grown locally.
5. Say no to plastic bags and use your own cloth bags instead.
6. Recycle as much of your rubbish as you can.
7. Reduce your shower time to 4 to 5 minutes a day.
8. Turn the tap off while you are brushing your teeth.
9. Always use both sides of a piece of paper and recycle it when you are done.
10. Plant a tree to soak up carbon dioxide from the atmosphere.

GLOSSARY

atmosphere - the cloud of gases that surrounds the planet and protects us from ultraviolet radiation from the sun, while also trapping some sunlight and making the planet suitable for life

average - the most common or usual

biomass - organic material made from plant and animal matter, including household and industrial waste, which stores energy that can be harnessed to produce electricity

carbon dioxide - a particularly potent greenhouse gas that is dramatically increasing due to human activity

carbon footprint - the amount of carbon dioxide produced by an individual, business or government; in Australia, each person produces approximately 19 tonnes of carbon dioxide every year

carbon sink - an organism that soaks up and stores carbon from the atmosphere, such as a tree

chlorofluorocarbon (CFC) - an artificial greenhouse gas used in aerosol cans, fridges, foam and some air conditioners, which can heat the atmosphere and destroy the ozone layer

climate - the average weather conditions over a long period of time

climate change - the process by which the overall climate varies between one temperature and a new average temperature

climatologist - a scientist who studies average weather patterns over long periods of time

deforestation - the widespread chopping down of trees and forest in order to create farmland or land for humans

drought - a period of little or no rainfall

electricity - a form of energy that results from the existence and movement of charged particles called electrons and protons

electricity grid - the system of connecting wires that transfers energy from power plants to homes and other locations

emissions - the release of greenhouse gases, such as carbon dioxide and methane, into the atmosphere

ossil fuels - ancient fossils from plants and animals that died millions of years ago, which vhen burned release the greenhouse gases stored within them

lobal warming - an increase in the overall climate of the planet caused by the release of reenhouse gases into the atmosphere

reenhouse gases - the invisible gases that make up the atmosphere and trap heat, including arbon dioxide, methane, hydrogen, nitrogen and oxygen

ydro-electricity - energy that uses the power of moving water to generate electricity

negawatt - 1000 kilowatts, which is enough electricity to run about 500 large family homes

neteorologist - a scientist who studies weather conditions, including rainfall, wind and xtreme weather events

nethane - a potent greenhouse gas produced by livestock when they expel gas and also ound in swampy areas and rubbish tips; also a fossil fuel

atural gas - a gaseous fossil fuel that is made up primarily of methane

uclear power - high levels of energy generated by splitting uranium-235 atoms and creating nuclear reaction

etroleum - a fossil fuel found deep beneath the Earth and the oceans, which is refined and sed to power cars and other forms of transport

hotovoltaic (PV) panels - flat reflective panels made up of many smaller solar cells that onvert the energy from the sun directly into electricity

adioactive waste - radiation left over from creating nuclear power; it is highly dangerous to ll forms of life and remains so for more than 10,000 years

olar power - energy generated from harnessing the power of the sun

ectonic plate - a segment of the Earth's crust that moves horizontally relative to other egments beneath the land surface; this can cause earthquakes

nequivocal - clear and plain

INDEX

FURTHER INFORMATION

Using the Internet

Explore the Internet to find out more about climate change, global warming and the alternative energies mentioned in this book. Keywords include 'climate change', 'global warming' and the names of people, places and events you are interested in.